Exeter
Yesterday & Today

PETER THOMAS

SUTTON PUBLISHING LIMITED

Sutton Publishing Limited
Phoenix Mill · Thrupp · Stroud
Gloucestershire · GL5 2BU

First published 2000

Copyright © Peter Thomas, 2000

Title page: The Tudor House, see page 109.

British Library Cataloguing in Publication Data
A catalogue record for this book is available from the
British Library.

ISBN 0-7509-2335-0

Typeset in 10.5/13.5 Photina.
Typesetting and origination by
Sutton Publishing Limited.
Printed and bound in England by
J.H. Haynes & Co. Ltd, Sparkford.

> # This book is
> # dedicated to Lorna

Left: For 2,000 years Exeter has been a walled city. Thankfully, approximately 75 per cent of the wall still remains. In the 1960s this remarkable survivor was threatened with partial demolition because of the construction of Western Way. A 25ft section was removed from the wall amid much protest. The well-known archaeologist Lady Aileen Fox spoke out against it: 'The City Wall section has been dismissed as inferior to anything else in the neighbourhood. Houses had concealed the wall which was 18ft high and 7ft wide and its facing stones are intact and it compared favourably.' Devon Archaeology urged preservation and suggested the road could be realigned, but the wall section was demolished together with many buildings around it. *Right*: The path of the city wall across Western Way is now followed by a footbridge opened in 1994. It is named after Exeter's twin town in Russia, Yaroslavl. Access to the footbridge is by a round tower that leads to the Cathedral and Quay car park. The military style tower gives an impression of an ancient fortress, reflecting, perhaps, Exeter's Roman past. Western Way bypass is now a major route through the city.

Contents

An aerial view of Exeter, *c.* 1927. Bedford Circus can clearly be seen in the centre of the photograph. The High Street's original width is seen throughout.

INTRODUCTION

The idea behind this book is to give an impression of Exeter's former buildings and historic sites and to compare them with what exists today. The images showing modern Exeter were taken when traffic was at a minimum so that buildings may be properly seen. Also, the views in the new photographs have been matched as accurately as possible to those in the old, but after all the changes to street patterns and complete removal of whole areas of townscape this has sometimes been difficult to achieve. A noticeable difference, and a welcome one, is the number of trees now planted around Exeter. Often, however, they do cover up ill-conceived buildings and sites.

There are sometimes misunderstandings about where certain buildings of note stood in the city. It is hoped, therefore, that this publication may prove useful and act as a street guide to the past. Any comments made are purely personal.

In 1886 in his book *Old Exeter* the architect James Crocker recorded the loss of seventeen historic buildings. Another eminent architect, Mr Harbottle Reed, read a paper to The Devonshire Association in 1931 entitled 'Demolition of ancient buildings of Exeter in the last half century'. The paper contains a list of thirty buildings plus historical and architectural features that had been removed, depleting the ancient fabric of the city. Demolition persisted until recent times, with the vast majority of later removals being undertaken by the local authority. The Second World War is often cited as the main reason for the loss of much of Exeter's heritage. However, in the postwar period a policy of removing anything old was adopted and much of the remaining ancient city was eradicated. It is interesting to follow the course of changes in the fabric of Exeter through the local newspapers of approximately the last fifty years.

In 1951 the Miles Memorial Clock Tower in Queen Street narrowly escaped demolition and 16 Edmund Street ('The House That Moved'), a fifteenth-century, timber-framed building, was threatened in 1955. The corner of Queen Street and High Street was also earmarked for removal. It included two of the city's finest historic buildings, 226 and 227 High Street. Only the façades of the two buildings were retained but then the corner of Queen Street was eventually demolished. A letter from a reader of the local newspaper in 1958 declared Exeter 'A City of Fools' for trying to destroy its heritage. He was commenting on another article written on the same subject nearly thirty years earlier!

In 1959 the charming row of Lants Almshouses in Bartholomew Street East was needlessly destroyed by the City Council in anticipation of a road-widening scheme. The project never transpired. Other almshouses were sensitively retained. The ruins of St Katherine's Almshouses had been attractively laid out as a memorial after the Blitz of 1942.

In 1961 the ancient area of Exe Island was to be radically changed by the creation of Western Way inner bypass. The late eighteenth-century stone arch, a feature of New Bridge Street, that led directly into the island, was replaced by an ugly concrete bridge which destroyed the attractive entrance. A short distance away at the corner of Frog Street,

16 Edmund Street made news worldwide when it was lifted from its original site and transported to the corner of West Street in 1961.

The Valiant Soldier public house located at the corner of Holloway Street and Magdalen Street was a focal point for the locality. The pub, together with Regency and earlier timber-framed buildings, created a fascinating townscape. All buildings were torn down to create Western Way inner bypass in 1962.

Exeter had a long history of theatre and the Theatre Royal in New North Road was one of the most prestigious in the country. Lack of support for the theatre presented developers with an opportunity and it was demolished in 1963.

In the postwar period changing street patterns also resulted in the loss of historic buildings. The restructuring of Paris Street wiped out the Axminster Inn at the junction with Russell Street. Its fate was sealed in 1964.

In the 1960s many properties in the city, regardless of their historical status, were subject to removal by the local authority or at the suggestion of developers. The prime High Street site of St Stephen's Church was viewed by a developer in 1965 with the intention of demolishing it and rebuilding on the site. The plan did not go ahead, but it was in this year that a scheme was proposed for the setting up of a maritime museum which would become a major tourist attraction. The project was to bring life back to the derelict Quay and Basin and find a new and appropriate role for the disused Victorian warehouses.

In 1965 the Elizabethan property 38 North Street, one of Exeter's architectural gems, was closed as part of the proposed 'Golden Heart' redevelopment project. In 1966 a shopping list report was brought out in the autumn relating to the project and in November consultants advised the City Council not to pull down the Civic Hall or Higher Market yet! Then in 1968 ambitious plans were launched which included the redevelopment of Waterbeer Street, Goldsmith Street and Pancras Lane. It proposed the retention of the Higher Market, which was to be altered to include an exhibition hall, gallery and hall seating 1,000 people. This idea, however, did not come to fruition. In 1969 final plans emerged to redevelop the 6½ acre site and create a new road system designed to serve Exeter up to the year 2010. Further proposals for the Guildhall Shopping Centre included the construction of a 100 room hotel on the north side and a tourist information centre, neither of which was realised. The Guildhall Shopping Centre project took thirty years to finalise. It resulted in one of the most scandalous planning decisions in Exeter – to remove the Elizabethan property at 38 North Street. The interior contained superb decorated plaster ceilings, murals, interior courtyard and balcony of the highest merit, all of which were needlessly destroyed. The building was recorded and demolished: the site then became the faceless west side of the Guildhall Shopping Centre.

By 1969 much work had been done to create the new Western Way inner bypass, which gave improved access across the River Exe to the west, and the new Exe Bridge North was duly opened on 30 July. In the city centre the corner site of Queen Street and High Street, latterly occupied by John Webber Sports, was leased to C&A for the creation of a new store. The proposal threatened the famous adjacent Tudor properties, but the company was obliged to retain the frontages, which had previously been the premises of The Western Times Company. It had been suggested that the whole section of the street at this point be removed.

The medieval Wynards Almshouses were owned by the well-known Kennaway family of Devon until 1950, when they were taken over by the Exeter Municipal Charities. By 1969 only two residents remained. Exeter City Council was approached when the charity decided to sell its interest in 1970. The organisation also suggested that these wonderful buildings be demolished. A grant of £4,000 was obtained from the Historic Buildings Council and a further £1,000 from the City Council to purchase the almshouses. The local authority instigated repairs and restoration and the buildings were converted for eight voluntary social service organisations at a further cost of £24,000. Today the almshouses are still a major part of Exeter's heritage. Also in 1970 parts of Alphington Street and Cowick Street were demolished to make way for the road system leading up to the new Exe Bridge. The ferry at the Quay was threatened with closure, and the Local Authority obtained an Act of Parliament to dismantle it. The service was stopped in 1972 but later resumed as a result of the intervention of the Maritime Museum.

One of Exeter's largest and most prominent buildings, the Royal Devon and Exeter Hospital in Southernhay, was closed in 1974 and recommendations were put forward to convert it into flats, but the plan failed to transpire. The Miles Memorial Clock Tower, in Queen Street, was listed in this year by the Department of the Environment as a building of special historical interest, thus securing its future.

The restoration of a seventeenth-century property in Tudor Street, Exe Island, took its owner Mr Bill Lovell twelve years to complete. In 1975 the Tudor House was offered to the City Council for £45,000 as a heritage and tourist attraction. The City Council refused the offer.

In 1976 controversial development to remove completely the top west corner of Queen Street (Walton's complex) again attracted media attention. The corner was designated for complete removal so that a new Marks & Spencer store could be built. Then in 1977 proposals were put forward to demolish a whole section of Magdalen Street to make way for part of the Western Way inner bypass.

In 1979 St Petrock's Church, no longer used for parish worship, faced an uncertain future. Fears were expressed that it would be removed to make way for commercial development. It was also in 1979 that the new riverside Shilhay Housing scheme was described as 'Blunderland' in a newspaper report. The City Council had proceeded with the project in the face of intense local criticism and pressure not to use the site for housing because of its proximity to the city's nightclubs. City Councillors ignored warnings from the *Express & Echo* newspaper, and large numbers of complaints were brought by the new tenants. Shilhay was awarded a medal for good design in housing by the Secretary of State for the Environment in 1979. A further nickname was given to the project by residents: 'Colditz'.

The completion of the new Marks & Spencer store at this time also prompted criticism. Commenting on the design, newspaper headlines read 'They could have done better'.

Work was also taking place in St Thomas to create a new leisure centre. The Plaza was opened in 1986 by HRH The Princess of Wales.

In 1985 the city's Archaeological Field Unit uncovered the original Elizabethan dock at Exeter Quay. The site became the Quay House Interpretation Centre after the transit shed was restored by the City Council. One year later nearby Cricklepit Mill, the only working mill left in the city, was put forward for a facelift that did not materialise.

In 1986 the ABC Cinema was demolished in High Street. In the same year a proposal to uncover the Roman Bath House in Cathedral Yard was put forward. Discovered in the early 1970s, this highly important site has still never been developed as an attraction.

Following many years of restoration work by English Heritage the medieval building of Bowhill on Dunsford Hill was opened to the public in 1996, and today is occupied by the Devonshire Association.

For many Exonians 1997 marks the loss of the city's prime attraction: the Maritime Museum. A breakdown between the museum and the City Council left the riverside venue deserted. No further attraction has been found to replace this unique collection of the world's working boats. A further loss at this time was the Art Deco building in Smythen Street, formerly built for Evans Gadd, the wholesale chemists. The building, which was on a prime site and could have been restored and used, was demolished. While one building was removed another was being restored, thanks to the tenacity and determination of a number of individuals. No. 21 Mint Lane, off Fore Street, was originally part of the eleventh-century St Nicholas Priory and is now well on the way to being fully restored. This important medieval building will contribute to the drive to retain Exeter's heritage.

In 1989 the site of Trew's Weir Mill downstream from the Quay was mostly cleared for housing. A new building was also constructed in Castle Street on the site of the old Castle Hotel and has added a new dimension and interest to this area.

At the beginning of the new millennium a number of projects are now proposed for Exeter, most importantly the highly controversial redevelopment of Princesshay and Bedford Street for new retail use. The project seeks to remove a massive part of the central area of the city and to reconstruct the site, but the move has provoked an unprecedented response from the citizens of Exeter, with the possibility of a public enquiry. Other recent proposals include a plan for the refurbishment of Cricklepit Mill and construction of new buildings on the site. This project has now started. Proposals for the building of a new hall of justice in Station Yard, Queen Street, and for the coach and bus station in Paris Street have now been put forward but have yet to be finalised.

Over the last fifty years no building has been erected in Exeter, apart from in Castle Street, that can be viewed as significantly heightening the architectural profile of the city. Decisions taken seem only to have looked to short-term financial gain with little idea of how best to utilise the city's historic setting. Exeter's heritage and history appear to have taken a back seat and lost priority. It is up to individuals to judge for themselves whether the continuing changes to Exeter's character are in fact creating a better and more interesting environment.

Peter Thomas
Exeter, September 2000

1

High Street from South Street to Eastgate, including Bedford Street

The north side of the upper High Street from the post office, *c.* 1935.

High Street after the major air raid of 4 May 1942. This is the central area after the remains of most buildings had been removed. The subsequent policy of demolishing some of the city's surviving historic buildings has been questioned ever since. To the south side of the cathedral gutted Bedford Chapel can be seen but the remains of Bedford Circus have already been demolished. Thomas Sharpe, who was commissioned to draw up a new plan for rebuilding the city, recommended that Bedford Circus be reconstructed but this idea was never adopted. The citizens of Exeter were to see fundamental changes to the character of the centre of the city which were alien to the kind of surroundings they had grown up in. The style and shape of the new, dominating, monolithic architecture swept away any feeling of the old city; between 1950 and 1965 the central area was a building site.

High Street from Boots the Chemist, March 2000. The entrance to Princesshay from High Street is seen on the left. It was approximately here that the entrance to the Eastgate Arcade stood. A large arched gateway with fine wrought-iron gates led to a glass-covered arcade which ended in a huge round stained-glass window. Some of Exeter's finest shops operated from the arcade. Today's Virgin Megastore is the approximate location of the post office, which occupied a substantial site. The High Street contained many historic and interesting buildings. Pre-war many shopkeepers took pride in their premises and promoted their history. Today the mixture of varying architecture, interesting streets and decorative shop façades has mostly been destroyed. At the beginning of the new millennium the future of the city centre is undecided.

High Street at its junction with South Street, North Street and Fore Street, *c*. 1935. At this time Hepworths the tailors occupied the shop on the corner of North Street and opposite was the Fifty Shilling Tailors. R.J. Woodley Shoes, Woolworth's and Moons were on the north side of the street. Milletts, the Ex-Government Stores, is shown on the right, and now trades from the corner of Goldsmith Street. Traffic was two-way through the whole of High Street.

This photograph of the junction of High Street with South Street today shows that two buildings have been lost from the corner with South Street and restoration of the façade of nos 70 and 71 (right, next to the church), has taken place. The street is now paved with sets and traffic is limited. The shopfront on the left (earlier Hepworths) does little to blend with the style of the original building shown above.

An interesting row of shopfronts appear in this photograph of 189 High Street upwards, *c.* 1935. Adjacent to R.J. Woodley's shoe shop (left) is the large shop of ironmongers Garton & King, established in 1700. The double-fronted premises had been extended in 1804 to include a foundry in Waterbeer Street. The company symbol, a Golden Hammer, is on the façade. Next door was Pinder & Tuckwell, the tailors, advertising itself as 'The home of real tailoring'. The shop entrance had a fine ironwork gate. No. 192 was the premises of Moons, specialists in pianos, radios and records. The famous symbol of HMV appears on the front of the building. The vintner Gilbey is next door.

Today the site of Garton & King, which traded here until 1933, is occupied by McDonald's and HMV in the premises purpose-built for Woolworth's in the mid-1930s. Many of the original decorative architectural features have been lost from this section of the street.

The junction of High Street and South Street, 1930s. The corner building was used by the Ocean Accident & Guarantee Corporation Ltd whose name stood out from the façade on the first floor. On the ground floor the well-known Exeter Company of Holman Ham conducted its business as a dispensing chemist. A tram traction pole has been converted to a lighting stand. Attached to the pole are some of the first traffic lights to be erected in Exeter.

Two buildings on the corner of South Street were lost in the blitz of 1942 and the site was rebuilt. They do not have the imposing presence of the previous buildings.

A horse-drawn bus passing the Guildhall with a heavy load of passengers on top and inside the vehicle, *c.* 1890. The street surface is quite rough and there is no sign of a motor car. The general scene is far less hurried than today.

The roadway at this part of High Street is now 50 per cent narrower than it was in 1890 and the pavements have been widened. Bollards have been erected to protect the Guildhall from accidental damage and to limit vehicles. Only buses and occasionally the Mayor's vehicle use the road. Unloading goods can, however, cause congestion. Beyond Goldsmith Street all buildings are new to the corner of Queen Street.

In the 1960s two-way traffic in High Street sometimes caused problems but not to the extent it would do today. This view was taken in 1964 from St Martin's Lane looking down the north side of High Street. These frontages were protected by preservation orders, but that did not save them from the new Marks & Spencer development, which altered one of the city's most sensitive sites in the late 1970s.

The shop in central High Street built for Marks & Spencer was highly controversial: it was a heavy fortress-like design and conglomeration of styles. The Queen Street façade, although a reconstruction of former buildings, took no account of previous shopfronts, reducing the interest in this sensitive part of the site. Extensive criticism was levelled at the new development. The influential *Architects Journal* described the £7 million store as 'A Dog's Dinner of a scheme'. It went on to state that 'bits and pieces of historic buildings, modern design and a range of grotesque pastiche are said to echo materials and forms already used in Exeter'. The City Council's Development Committee and the Civic Society stated that on the whole they were pleased with it.

High Street, seen at its junction with Queen Street, had a far more sympathetic style in 1964 than it does today. Upper Queen Street had an elegant and substantial façade that extended from Little Queen Street to High Street, the rounded corner joining the older buildings smoothly.

The reconstruction of this corner had a significant impact on the whole feel of central High Street: the resulting C&A building proved to be one of the worst examples of architecture in the city.

This charming photograph, *c.* 1910, shows the busy junction of Queen Street with High Street and a number of horse-drawn vehicles unloading goods for retailers. The main subjects of the photograph are two timber-framed buildings dating from 1564, 41 and 42 High Street. At this period, no. 41 was under the ownership of Hinton Lake, chemist, and no. 42 *The Western Times*, with its city advertisement office on the ground floor. Hinton Lake took over both properties and became one of Exeter's most renowned businesses. On its closure in 1970, these prestigious buildings were acquired by Laura Ashley; their marvellous restoration is still a joy to behold.

Nos 41 and 42 High Street have been sympathetically restored: the ground floor is integrated with its upper storeys. Developers of other premises in Exeter have not adopted this approach. In recent years the City Council has produced a special booklet on designing shopfronts as a guide for shop owners, but despite local authority efforts the city still has classic examples of poor shopfront design, which downgrade Exeter's historical status.

Nos 41 and 42 High Street, c. 1915. For a very long time these buildings were the property of Hinton Lake, chemists. The two timber-framed structures were said to have been erected in 1564 and a carved door head used to bear this date. It is now in the City Museum. The buildings were to be restored in 1983–4. Other discoveries have been made on the site including part of a Roman road relating to Exeter's Roman fortress. Ancient fireplaces have been found in the walls, and a newel staircase has also been uncovered. An exciting discovery was traces of sixteenth-century wall painting, now protected. The photograph shows that at this time no. 42 was under the management of the City & County Cycle Depot.

Nos 41 and 42 High Street are now joined as one building and were extensively restored in 1983–4. The quality of restoration has ensured a high profile for this very important site.

This delightful picture, dating from *c.* 1930, shows the north side of High Street from Queen Street upwards, including Boots, the *Express & Echo* and *Western Morning News* offices, J. & G. Ross, tailors and Timothy White. Despite some variance in age, the buildings formed a cohesive group that was one of the High Street's prominent architectural features. Nos 225 and 226 were a pair of timber-framed buildings dating from the sixteenth and seventeenth centuries; they were historically significant. The shopfronts are later in date but have been sensitively designed to blend with the upper storeys. The rounded double windows of Ross, the tailor's, were a particular feature in Exeter.

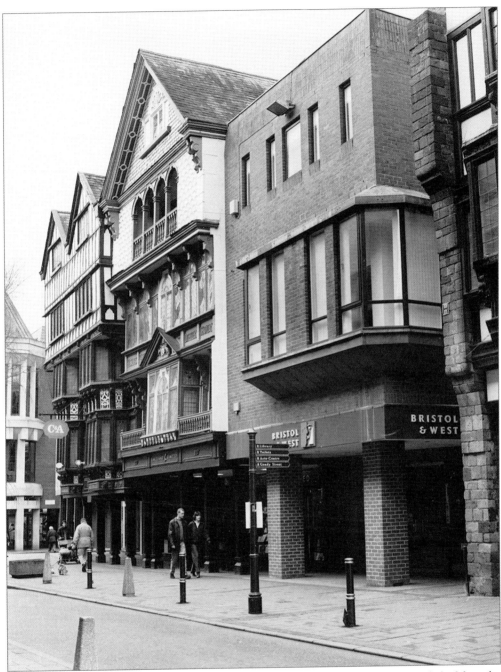

Today the site has greatly changed. Timothy White's building was totally demolished but the replacement jars against its neighbours. The interiors of nos 225/226 and 227 were destroyed with only the façades left for posterity. In order to retain the frontages, steel girders have been used at ground level as supports. These beautiful examples of sixteenth- and seventeenth-century work were not even integrated into the new rear structures. It is an alarming example of the failure to protect all aspects of our historic buildings. Perhaps only by good luck we still have these superb examples of craftsmanship. The whole of this section of High Street was also threatened with demolition in the past.

The north side of central High Street from Commercial Union (no. 240) to London Inn Square, *c.* 1935. Before the Second World War differing styles of buildings lined the street and their often sumptuous interiors included major historical features. The railed frontage of the Commercial Union dominated and King Alfred's statue looked down from above the entrance on passers-by. Next door Bruford's not only sold jewellery but also specialised in old furniture. The huge exterior clock was carved by Harry Hems, the famous Exeter ecclesiastical sculptor, whose studio was in Longbrook Street. The adjacent buildings of Fred Ford Signs and Wippell Bros & Row were timber fronted. These three shops created a prominent group of fine buildings. The Devon and Somerset Stores next door was brick built with some excellent decorative work, including a row of arched windows on the first floor and a top balustrade with finials. The British Shoe Company was plain but had a good shopfront. It abutted the ancient church of St Lawrence whose porch held a figure of Elizabeth I. Next to the church was the Empire cinema.

Exeter's upper High Street is 50 per cent wider today than it was before the Second World War and is closed to all traffic except buses. After the last war it opened to two-way traffic. In recent years there has been great debate as to whether Exeter should be totally pedestrianised, but as yet no firm decision has been made. The redeveloped High Street is virtually devoid of any interesting architectural features and the rebuilding of the central area has been the subject of consternation ever since its inception. In the last twenty years the local authority has tried to break the monotony by installing seats, flower beds and signposts.

One of the most impressive façades to be found in High Street was that of nos 238–40, the Commercial Union Assurance Company, seen here in about 1910. The frontage incorporated eight Corinthian columns supporting a balconied portico on which stood a large statue of Alfred the Great, the company's symbol. Two fine gas lamps and ornate railings completed the design. The portico still stood after the Exeter blitz of May 1942 after other buildings had been removed. It was a sad end to a fine building.

The site today has little to commend it. At this point in High Street the road was pushed back, widening the street by approximately 50 per cent.

High Street in about 1925 with the dominant focal point of St Lawrence's Church – the Empire cinema is next door. Tramlines ran down the street and the road was paved with stone sets. Numerous shop blinds extended to the kerb edge. A tram traction pole crossed the middle of the street. On the right-hand side the turning into Bedford Street, which is deceptively narrow, can be seen. In this photograph only one open-top car is seen and a horse-drawn covered wagon and hand cart stand outside the church. The street was the same width as it had been for centuries, right up to the London Inn Square.

Today the site of St Lawrence's Church is marked by a plaque on the outside of the Co-operative Bank entrance on the left, adjacent to Down to Earth. The church stood much further forward than the current shops and at the rear was a small graveyard. Entry was through a small iron gate fronting a passageway in High Street. It would be interesting to ask those working in the bank today whether they have ever felt ill at ease in their building, which covers a burial ground!

High Street from the Devon & Somerset Stores to Queen Street, *c.* 1935. This view from the corner of Bedford Street shows High Street at its original width, with two-way traffic. Traffic lights operated just outside Wippell Bros & Row and the cars are waiting for the lights to change. Shown clearly down the street are the premises of Eland, the bookseller, whose advert extends down the full height of the building. The company had a fine interior gallery and balcony.

The destruction of the city during the Second World War necessitated the complete rebuilding of the central area. Today's view from Bedford Street westwards clearly shows the north side of High Street constructed much farther back from where the earlier pre-war buildings had stood. The whole side of 229 High Street was left exposed, creating an eyesore. In recent times this space has been used for a mural depicting historical Exeter characters, but there is no plaque to indicate to interested parties what the work shows. The characters are in fact Sir Thomas Bodley (1544–1613), Nicholas Hilliard, the famous miniaturist (1547–1619) and Princess Henrietta (1644–70). The personalities, all of whom have links with Exeter, were chosen as the subjects as the result of a competition held by the City Council. The mural was finished in October 1991.

High Street from opposite the Empire cinema. A lady reads a billboard outside the picture house. Railings that extended the length of St Lawrence's Church were removed for the war effort. Its porch, incorporating the statue of Elizabeth I, was built in 1694 from the remains of the old conduit in High Street. After the blitz of May 1942 the church still stood but was later demolished. The historic statue was acquired by an Exeter company who proudly displayed it before returning it to the city in 1993 and today is seen at the entrance to the underground passages. On the left of the photograph are the premises of Joshua Daw, tailor, next to Freeths Tofferies and the Motor Union Insurance Co. Ltd. The domed roof of Dellers Café is seen protruding into High Street on the corner of Bedford Street.

Central High Street is lacking in interest today. Exeter has lost its soul to commercial activities. The postwar redevelopment failed to include living accommodation in the central area, the result being that it becomes a ghost town in the evenings. The demolition of the Theatre Royal in the 1960s also took its toll on the diminishing social life. In very recent years the local authority has tried to reverse the situation by bringing more pressure to utilise redundant buildings in the centre of Exeter.

The north side of the upper High Street from the post office, *c.* 1935. This view from Eastgate looking down High Street shows, on the right, the building from which Mark Rowe & Sons ran its business. The shop windows on the ground floor were some of Exeter's most unusual: they were double concave and were quite unique to the company. On the right is the bronze wall plaque that is today displayed opposite Boots the Chemist. It details the demolition of East Gate in 1784. The frontage of Mark Rowe's was created from stone taken from the old city gate and the statue of Henry VII was incorporated into the façade. The statue had been a feature of the Eastgate. Adjacent to Mark Rowe's was the Apothecaries Hall, an interesting building with a noticeboard stating 'established in 1789'. Its neighbour, John's Tea Importers, operated from a building with the date AD 1297 clearly painted on the front. The building was probably seventeenth century, however. Standing in the street is a horse-drawn carrier belonging to Sutton & Co., couriers, which operated from Victoria Yard, Queen Street.

By the end of 1961 Eastgate corner had been completely rebuilt. The temporary shops that had been erected on what is now the top of Princesshay and Eastgate House in 1948–9 to keep business flowing were demolished. For those who remembered the old High Street, the newly built shops presented a startling change in character, bearing no resemblance to what was there before.

The Eastgate Arcade, *c.* 1940. This was a much talked about feature in High Street, a premier shopping location. Constructed in 1882, it was the home of noted Exeter companies. In 1939 these included jewellers, drapers, art furnishers, a photographic studio, antique dealer, coal merchants, knitwear shop, optical company, hairdresser, chemists, Cripples Aid Home Industry, refrigerator manufacturers, wool shop, umbrella makers and the Newfoundland Fish Company. The arcade was often decorated with flowers. In the postwar period Exeter gained itself a reputation as a floral city thanks to the City Engineer John Brierley, who instigated the installation of flower beds across the city.

The destruction of the Eastgate Arcade during the blitz in May 1942 robbed Exeter of its prestigious glass-covered arcade and the fine round stained-glass window constructed at its east end. Princesshay replaced the old Arcade but has never achieved the status of its predecessor. The new shopping area was not covered over and it lacks intimacy. Today the removal of Princesshay is being planned.

Eastgate at the junction with London Inn Square, *c.* 1930. On the left-hand side the entrance to the Eastgate Arcade can be seen. The clock above the entrance shows 8.30 a.m. and at night it was illuminated. The arched gateway, made from red sandstone, was carved with the words 'Eastgate Arcade'. A decorative metal gate closed off the arcade at night. Adjacent is the National Provincial Bank. The substantial and imposing building next door is the post office. Construction started in 1881 and the building opened in 1883. After the Second World War the post office moved to Bedford Street.

On the left of this photograph is Eastgate House and in front of it is a granite standing stone bearing the bronze plaque once attached to the wall of Mark Rowe & Sons. The road narrows at this point to slow buses down and allow pedestrians to cross safely. Since the Second World War the High Street has undergone a number of changes, including a one-way traffic system, subsequently changed to two way. The roadway was then narrowed by 50 per cent and access was limited to buses. Total pedestrianisation is now being considered.

Bruford & Son, 241 High Street, c. 1930. The company specialised in old English silver, antique
furniture and works of art. The double-gabled premises may originally have been two buildings, as
seen elsewhere in Exeter. The company took a particular interest in Exeter silver spoons and in
1913 invited inspection of a range of these rare items. The most striking feature of the premises
was its huge wooden clock supported on the back of Old Father Time. The clock was skilfully
executed by the ecclesiastical sculptor Harry Hems. The clock shows this photograph was taken at
1.46 p.m. To the left of Bruford's is part of the frontage of the Commercial Union building.

No clock exists on the site of Bruford's today but people are killing time waiting for buses.

Bruford's famous clock carved by the sculptor Harry Hems of Exeter. This selection of photographs gives an indication of the type of interiors that existed pre-war in Exeter. Some of Exeter's business premises contained interesting historical and architectural details. (*Bruford's of Exeter*)

Originating from Eastbourne, jeweller Ernest Bruford took over 241 High Street from Pipers jewellers (established 1721). The impressive High Street property was originally the town house for the Earls of Morley. It provided a fine showroom for the company. Bruford's also took over Ellett Lake & Son, jewellers, at 43 High Street in 1924. No. 241 High Street was destroyed in the bombing of 1942 and the company moved to Central Station and in 1957 to 1 Bedford Street. In 2000 the company has only just moved to 17 Guildhall Shopping Centre after forty-three years in Bedford Street. (*Bruford's of Exeter*)

The interior staircase at Bruford's. (*Bruford's of Exeter*)

Antique furniture for sale at Bruford's. (*Bruford's of Exeter*)

The Castle Hotel, Castle Street, 1937. Before the Second World War Castle Street, leading from High Street, was much narrower than today. At the junction of Castle Street and Old Castle Street was the Castle Hotel, taking its name from Rougemont Castle a short distance up the road. The hotel was a favourite haunt of solicitors and barristers who attended the Assize Courts, and members of Devon County Council, whose headquarters were in the castle. The hotel was destroyed in 1942 during the Exeter blitz. For many years huge timbers supported the adjacent buildings.

In 1961 the timbers were replaced and to make the site more attractive Virginia creeper was planted to cover it – in autumn this was a vibrant attraction. The new building of 1989 has added another dimension to the street, being one of the few modern buildings in the central area to add to the city's appeal. Opened in 1990, it is occupied by a high-class jeweller. Such inspiration has been sorely lacking in Exeter: far more could be done to enhance existing buildings and difficult sites.

The newly constructed building in Castle Street.

The entrance to Castle Street from High Street, *c.* 1930. This stretch of road was far narrower pre-war than it is today. A car is seen turning right into Old Castle Street. At this time Bailey Street did not exist; it was created after the Second World War to make a quick exit into Queen Street from New North Road. The National Westminster Bank is seen on the left and opposite is Charles & Charles, bootmakers.

The view from High Street shows the new building that has now replaced the Castle Hotel. The site became a well-known feature of the city as the adjacent building had to be shored up with huge timbers to prevent collapse.

Bedford Circus, *c.* 1915. Before the Second World War Exeter had two dominant architectural features, the cathedral and Bedford Circus. Recognised as one of the finest Georgian crescents in England, Bedford Circus was constructed on the site of Bedford House, formerly the site of a Dominican convent. The well-proportioned circus, consisting of fine houses, a chapel on the west side, and a central oval garden, was constructed by builder Robert Stribling. The foundation stone was laid on 27 May 1773 but the project was not completed for another fifty years. It offered the most prestigious private dwellings in the city. This photograph looks towards its northern aspect and central garden. The creeper-covered façades enclosed simple Georgian porticoes. Bedford Circus was a pick-up point for horse cabs and a cabbies' box is seen behind the ornamentally railed statue of William Reginald Courtenay, Earl of Devon. Although blitzed, sections of the circus remained standing, but were later demolished. Rebuilding would have been an option. The mature garden trees, the last remnants of Bedford Circus, were removed in 1951.

Bedford Street. In earlier times the entrance to Bedford Circus was narrow but it was widened in the nineteenth century. The postwar rebuilding of Bedford Street saw the construction of a wide road laid out further to the west than the old one. It crossed over part of the site of Dellers Café, previously blitzed. A commemorative feature marking the rebuilding of the area and the construction of Princesshay was opened by HRH Princess Elizabeth on 21 October 1949. The building of Princesshay took approximately twelve years, and by 1962 the new shopping complex and Bedford Street were complete. Today the street has been narrowed and is utterly different to the elegant pre-war site.

A corner of Bedford Circus from the entry with Southernhay looking east, 1938. The properties at this time were occupied by solicitors, stockbrokers, the National Liberal Organisation and, shown clearly at no. 12, the Bedford Car Washing Agency. The company advertises 'repairs, washing and greasing'. Its extensive garage was situated at the rear of the circus.

Where part of the city's finest Georgian circus once stood we now have the general post office.

Martin's Bank and Barclays Bank on the east side of Bedford Street, 1939. This prominent site, purchased in 1882 for £2,250, became the headquarters of the Exeter Conservatives, called the Constitutional Club. For its opening on 16 January 1884 huge celebrations were held, and the High Street decorated and illuminated. The premises were later adapted for other purposes. The ground floor was taken over by Martin's Bank which insensitively altered the Bedford Street frontage in 1939. The High Street corner received the same treatment from Barclays Bank.

The post-war replacement, looking towards High Street from Bedford Street.

The Theatre Royal, Bedford Street, *c.* 1900. The history of Exeter theatres is a tragic one. The building shown is the second theatre on the site; its predecessor had been destroyed by fire. This building also caught fire in 1885 and the photograph was taken shortly after. A new theatre was built at the junction of Longbrook Street and New North Road (*see* page 56), but it too suffered the ravages of fire in 1887.

The site of the old theatre at the end of Bedford Street is nondescript today. There should be some recognition of the fact that Exeter's early theatre stood there.

Above: Deller's Café seen from High Street, 1930s. The corner site of High Street with Bedford Street, west side, was to become one of the most well-known pre-war businesses in Exeter. The site had been the Half Moon Hotel but this was demolished in the early twentieth century and replaced by Lloyds Bank. The extensive site allowed the building of Dellers Café above and to the side of the bank, with the entrance in Bedford Street. This café became the focal point for social events in Exeter. The interior was the most lavish in the city, having an almost theatrical ambience with a

tiered dining-room with elaborate decorated plasterwork, drapes, private alcoves and often an orchestra played on the ground floor. Much of the building was destroyed by incendiaries in 1942, but its shell stood and was so well constructed that knocking it down proved difficult. Here was another a prime example of a building that could have been retained and restored; but it was demolished. The loss of Deller's is still regretted by many Exeter citizens. *Left*: The new building took on the monotonous style of the rest of the rebuilt street, which, unlike its predecessor, has no character. It is a very poor substitute for the well-built imposing structure that led to one of Exeter's architectural masterpieces, Bedford Circus.

St John's School (Blue Coat School), *c. 1930*. For many people it may come as a surprise that the upper section of Princesshay was once a substantial playground belonging to St John's School. This photograph shows one of the two large late nineteenth-century school buildings. It stood on the south side of the site, backing up to the city wall. The terraces in Southernhay can just be seen, along with the spire of the Congregational church. The entrance to the playground and school were directly off the High Street. The original High Street school building, converted from a hospital in the early seventeenth century, was demolished in 1880. The buildings shown were redundant from 1931 when the school closed.

Princesshay today is being considered for demolition as part of a major rebuilding project for the central area of Exeter. Public opinion is much stronger than it once was and enormous interest has been generated, expressing concerns about large-scale demolition and rebuilding.

2

The Sidwell Street Area

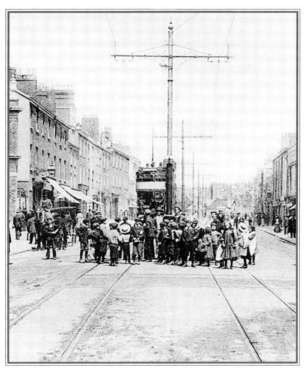

Upper Sidwell Street, *c.* 1910.

It is difficult to believe that this photograph shows Sidwell Street from the corner of London Inn Square when one compares it with the scene today. A large section of Sidwell Street survived the blitz but was to be bulldozed in the name of progress during postwar redevelopment. Sidwell Street was a busy thoroughfare with a large population living in close proximity. The demolition of houses between this main street and Newtown destroyed a vital element of the city centre and properties were not rebuilt. A wide variety of small shops lined the whole of Sidwell Street before its demise. Today it is merely utilitarian.

The view looking towards Sidwell Street today. On the immediate left is the site where the ABC cinema recently stood. This area was essentially London Inn Square, taking its name from the prominent hotel that stood on the site until February 1936. When the city was rebuilt in the '50s a plan to turn this area into a huge sunken garden with the traffic flowing round it was considered but abandoned. The Debenham's store, opened in March 1964, was originally constructed for Bobby's. It is one of Exeter's greatest eyesores and was voted Exeter's worst building in a newspaper poll in recent years.

The original entrance to Southernhay East from Sidwell Street, *c.* 1930. With the change of road pattern after the Second World War, this entry into Southernhay East no longer existed. Paris Street was also altered and widened. On the left is the Bude Hotel which extended to the corner of old Paris Street. The Southernhay Pharmacy, operated by Holman Ham the chemists, led into Southernhay East. The large central site was to be removed and rebuilt for L.H. Fearis Ltd, provision merchants.

The Fearis building escaped total destruction from the blitz and later became the Exeter Co-op. The building has been greatly altered internally but the exterior still reflects the 1930s style; it is now occupied by Next.

Exeter's Theatre Royal, built in 1889, stood on the corner of Longbrook Street and New North Road. The building shown in this 1930s picture was a replacement for the theatre that had been destroyed by fire two years earlier. For over seventy years the Theatre Royal was the hub of the community and many important actors and actresses played at this well-known venue. Postwar, the theatre found it difficult to make ends meet and started to show films. The decline in interest for live theatre created an opportunity for redevelopment and in 1963 the building was demolished.

The busy junction of Longbrook Street and New North Road is now dominated by a large office block called Portland House. While a theatre was created on the campus of Exeter University, it has never prompted the feeling that existed for the old Theatre Royal. Today there is a revival in live theatre and constant requests for a new theatre in the city centre.

Trams in Sidwell Street, *c.* 1930. The Pinhoe Road tram halts to allow a second to continue down the street to High Street. The two properties immediately to the left are the approximate sites of the Pram and Toy Shop today (closed in September 2000 after ninety-two years of trading). Many of the buildings shown were still in existence after the war, particularly on the north side of the street. The new era was to see the removal of a fascinating part of the townscape. In 1931 the trams stopped operating, but the traction poles were to be seen some time after and were often adapted for lighting.

The postwar rebuilding of Sidwell Street created an area with little of interest and nothing of architectural merit. The appalling façade of the Iceland building together with Tesco now forms a huge uncompromising barrier running up the north side of the street. The only interesting feature is a figure of St Sidwell (Exeter's patron saint) created on the Tesco façade, but the onlooker is not told what it is or why it is there. Tesco take note!

Upper Sidwell Street, with a large group of children probably waiting to board a tram, c. 1910. Sidwell Street, like many of Exeter's older roads, had numerous courts and alleyways, and today there are still a few of these in existence. In this part of Sidwell Street the double tram traction poles ran up the middle of the road. On the immediate left is the front of Sandow's Duke of York, the well-known pub, and the prominent frontage of the Methodist church. Opened in 1905, the church is one of the earliest examples of a building constructed using reinforced concrete.

Much of upper Sidwell Street is still intact and the Duke of York pub has been completely refurbished in recent years. Sidwell Street Methodist church has also been renovated and its charming dome is now illuminated, adding a new dimension to the street at night. Dominating the north side of the street is the Odeon cinema; it was built on the site of a demolished row of shops. The cinema was opened in 1937 and has been criticised for its overbearing size.

The end of Sidwell Street at the junction with Old Tiverton Road, *c.* 1910. A cabbies' box stood a short distance from the arched entrance of St Anne's Almshouses and Chapel. A number of these boxes were found across the city: they allowed the drivers to rest and pick up clients. In front of the box is a stone drinking trough for horses. Locally called the Fountain, the trough has now been relocated to the middle of a garden above the public toilets in Blackboy Road. It was paid for by lady supporters of the RSPCA and dedicated to Exeter surgeon Arthur Kempe, whose name is inscribed upon it.

Today the former site of Arthur Kempe's drinking trough is part of a busy roundabout for traffic flowing in and out of the city, and the site of the cabbies' box is an island for traffic bollards.

The Acland Hotel at the junction of Sidwell Street and York Road, *c.* 1930. Sidwell Street used to be full of small shops and businesses, pubs and hotels. This photograph shows one of the smaller hotels typical of old Exeter. The Acland Hotel, 57 Sidwell Street, was in a good position for passing trade and was just a short distance from the city centre. The hotel also had a saloon bar on the ground floor. The name was taken from the Acland family, the famous Devon landowners. The hotel stood at the junction with York Road and was destroyed by fire and high explosives in 1942. It was later the site of Eveleigh's Garage.

In March 2000 the site of 57 Sidwell Street was rebuilt as a twenty-four-hour shop, post office and flats. The corner site has thankfully been more sympathetically designed than many of its neighbours. Most of Sidwell Street today offers no more than purely functional buildings and the area, including the bus and coach station, has the potential for quality redevelopment. The postwar demolition of a number of interesting buildings in this busy thoroughfare destroyed most of the character of the street.

3

Queen Street, Gandy Street, Bartholomew Street & Smythen Street

Nos 15 and 16 Queen Street, *c.* 1933.

The corner of Queen Street and High Street, *c.* 1920. This was an elegant junction with an extensive façade running up the east side of Queen Street. It graciously curved into the High Street to join its older neighbours. Built in the mid-nineteenth century, the premises gave the appearance of being one building. Strict conditions applied to these buildings, stating that at no time could market produce be sold from the site, as this would have jeopardised business at the Higher Market. The building remained until 1970 and could have been retained, but everything was demolished.

The C&A store, built in 1973, is a blight on the city centre. Its monolithic style with slitted but windowless walls is a visual insult to its older neighbours.

In 1969 the entrance to Little Queen Street still retained part of the original Queen Street façade. The properties at 93 and 94 Queen Street were a tobacconist and a sports shop. Behind this frontage was the printing works of James Townsend & Sons, a well-known Exeter company. The Townsend premises were brick built and bore similarities to buildings found in old Goldsmith Street. They had interesting turrets, relief plaster work and decorative gables. All properties were demolished shortly after this picture was taken.

The rear of the C&A store replaces a range of varied buildings in Little Queen Street, one of our older side streets.

Queen Street from Higher Market to the Rougemont Hotel, *c.* 1910. At this time flower stalls on the outside of the market were a common sight. Internally it was laid out as an open pannier market with meat, fish, vegetables, dairy products. A shop had been created within the façade occupied by Hussey & Son. An interesting adjacent building was on the corner of Queen Street and Paul Street and was owned by Carr & Quick, wine merchants. On the opposite corner was the Museum Hotel, which took its name from the Royal Albert Memorial Museum. It was demolished so that Paul Street could be widened, to allow a greater flow of traffic.

Today the Higher Market has been radically altered but its frontage has been restored. The building owned by Carr & Quick was demolished and the site of the Museum Hotel is now a new business called Chandni Chowk, specialists in foreign clothes and artefacts.

The Higher Market, Queen Street, 1938. Exeter's Higher Market was a focal point for many people who came into the city to buy fish, meat, eggs, vegetables, flowers and other products. It had operated since 1838 and was constructed to clear the streets of stalls. The huge frontage is the largest structure of its type in Exeter. The market is shown with flower stalls outside; integrated into the façade were a number of shops. On the left is Quick & Co., leather merchants, and in the centre section Greenslades Tours, next to Madame James. The high shop windows retain the dignity of the façade. In September 1962 the Higher Market was closed and left abandoned for a number of years.

The creation of the Guildhall Shopping Centre in the 1970s removed all the structures surrounding the Higher Market but the main hall and Queen Street façade survived. The back of the market was fundamentally changed with the loss of the rear stepped entrance when the ground level was raised over 6ft. Goldsmith Street was obliterated and a golden opportunity to use one of our ancient streets as a tourist attraction was totally lost. Thankfully the front of the market was preserved but the concrete infilling has destroyed some of the elegance of the structure. The three blocked-in sections have removed light from the entrance and serve no real purpose.

Nos 15 and 16 Queen Street were the premises of Carr & Quick, a long-established Exeter wine and spirit merchants seen here *c.* 1933. At this time the first floor was occupied by Eagle, Star and British Dominions Insurance Co. Ltd. To the left Hussey & Son, estate agents and auctioneers, occupied a shop that was integrated into the façade of the Higher Market. To the right of Carr & Quick and in Paul Street is the arched side entrance to the Civic Hall, and beside it St Paul's Church (removed in 1936).

In Exeter there are a number of examples of replica frontages that have been created from concrete; to the onlooker they appear no different from the original. But the construction of the Guildhall Shopping Centre and the demolition of a large central area from Queen Street to North Street exhibited an insensitive approach to this important townscape. The style of the Carr & Quick building could have been replicated and successfully integrated into any new development. The new building lacked the style of its predecessor and the overbearing structure has marred the site.

Gandy Street in 1979; at this time it was a neglected back street. In earlier times it had been used by leather workers and it was to have a considerable face-lift after this date. The idea was to update the street, bringing back some of its character. Gandy Street contains some very nice period properties and its close proximity to High Street makes it a fascinating detour. The redevelopment had the support of the local retailers and today Gandy Street has a distinctive and appealing feel. The road was to be resurfaced with stone sets, which reflected the open gutters of earlier periods. It also become traffic free. Good quality shops operate in this street and during the summer it is festooned with flowers.

Gandy Street is now thriving, with constant attention being paid to the state of its buildings and general appearance. Such enhancement schemes are very reliant on good relationships between retailers and the local authority.

Evans, Gadd & Co. Ltd, Smythen Street, *c.* 1930. Until 1999 a substantial building existed in Smythen Street. It had previously been the premises of Evans, Gadd & Co. Ltd, wholesale chemists recorded as being in Fore Street earlier in the century. The company built this large Art Deco property in the 1920s and it was a model for other developments of its time. The spacious building, together with adjacent land comprising some 40,000 square feet, was sold in 1995 to a developer. The prominent site was ideal for leisure, a large-covered market or even a large-scale antiques centre. But the building was demolished.

The barred, brick-built replacement for the Evans, Gadd building is now a refuge for those with social problems and the intimidating look of the building does little to enhance the street. The refurbishment of the previous building could have provided the city with a much needed cultural centre or leisure facility, and at the same time could have highlighted the architectural merit of the area. The remaining open site will now be developed for housing.

One of the most delightful groups of buildings in Exeter was Lants Almshouses in Bartholomew Street East, seen here in about 1930. The row of brick-built properties was constructed by Richard Lant in 1763. The almshouses were built on top of the city wall and overlooked the yard of the Crown & Sceptre Hotel (today called the City Gate). A stone plaque on the front of the houses related their history. The buildings formed a community in their own right and added to the character of the street.

In the 1950s the City Council decided to create a major road through the area of Bartholomew Street, and destroyed the row of almshouses. The road traffic scheme never transpired but the city lost part of its heritage: the site today is an insignificant garden.

4

Goldsmith Street, Waterbeer Street & Paul Street

Waterbeer Street, 1959.

The Old Wool Hall, 22 Goldsmith Street, 1979. This was one of the more unusual buildings in the street. It belonged to the Exeter company of Lear, Browne & Dunsford. The five-arched building resembled earlier wool halls that had existed in Exeter but with open arcades. Built of Beer stone, the hall was probably constructed in the early to mid-nineteenth century and its design was unique in the city. At the time this picture was taken it was occupied by Laing Development, which was responsible for the construction of the new Marks & Spencer building. Virtually the whole of Goldsmith Street was to be destroyed with the building of the Guildhall Shopping Centre and the Marks & Spencer store.

A rare interior view of the Wool Hall, Goldsmith Street, gives an indication of its internal design. It was panelled in pine and large shelves extended from floor to ceiling, designed to hold large bolts of cloth. The building retained all its original gas light fittings. It was probably one of the last fully functional buildings of its period left in Exeter. The building was sold and demolished, and the stone from its frontage was given to the cathedral to assist with restoration.

Most people who use the entrance to Marks & Spencer from Goldsmith Street have no idea that the structure they pass through relates to an earlier building. To placate the city, the design for the new Marks & Spencer store had to take previous older structures into account and so a replica of the old Wool Hall was constructed. While well executed, the detail of the rosettes in line with the balustrading is not correct: the originals were all different. A further reconstruction was the gable of the Phoenix Inn (shown partly on the left). It originally stood to the right of the Wool Hall. For the onlooker this corner of the city is now a strange amalgam of styles, with no indication of how the mixture has been arrived at.

Waterbeer Street is shown after the demolition of the police station and looking towards the original properties in Goldsmith Street, 1979. Marks & Spencer had expressed interest in the retention of these properties but the whole group was removed.

The rebuilt corner site of Goldsmith Street as seen today. It does not seem logical to demolish existing standing structures which could be adapted and retained, but it is even more curious a decision to reinstate them in concrete.

Goldsmith Street at the junction with Waterbeer Street, *c.* 1960. On the left just after Lisles, the jeweller, is the entrance to Waterbeer Street with Stillmans the butchers. The street at this time contained a variety of older buildings and trades. One of Exeter's most ancient thoroughfares, it was home to hairdressers, printers, estate agents, accountants, a TV hire firm, fruit stores, tin plate works, grocers, St John Ambulance, tobacconists, handicraft shop, an inn, Exeter Chamber of Trade and, of course, Waltons store. The rear, stepped entrance of the Higher Market formed part of the side of the street.

Goldsmith Street has been virtually eliminated. The restoration and integration of the old street into the redevelopment scheme would have added a fascinating dimension to the project. However, the design ultimately used shows there was a determination to remove anything old. If the concept of retaining the frontage of the Wool Hall and other buildings had been more widely adopted, the whole feeling of Goldsmith Street would have been reinstated.

Goldsmith Street from the Paul Street end towards High Street, *c.* 1963. On the left the side of the Higher Market is just visible. The street was intact in 1963 and could have been renovated to become a popular thoroughfare. Today there is a distinct move to provide smaller shop units in the city to make shopping more appealing, as seen in Gandy Street. The wholesale removal of areas around the city centre like Goldsmith Street has resulted in a bland and often uninspired city centre.

Standing in the square at the Guildhall Shopping Centre after leaving the Market Arcade, the visitor is confronted by some of the most unimaginative architecture in the city. Moves are being made to revamp the area of the Guildhall Shopping Centre and if the project transpires it will make the site more acceptable. When one considers what could have been achieved if Goldsmith Street had been retained and what we have today, it is an extremely sad reflection on how Exeter's development has been handled in the postwar period. Guildhall Square was created by raising the ground level nearly 6ft, in the course of which the rear railed steps up to the Market entrance were destroyed. As an architectural feature in its own right the Higher Market could have been made much more impressive.

Waterbeer Street (the street of the Waterbearer's), 1959. This busy back street ran parallel with High Street. It included some prominent buildings, notably the Victorian Gothic police station, opened in 1887. A substantial brick building with a conical tower on the corner of St Pancras Lane, it was demolished, together with adjoining buildings, in the 1960s. Today only its foundation stone remains as part of a nondescript garden to remind us of its presence. In 1955 the adjacent buildings, nos 8, 9 and 10, were used as the Court House Annexe.

The opening of the Guildhall Shopping Centre in 1976 marked the end of the old heart of the city. The huge development had successfully removed all vestiges of a very ancient part of Exeter, apart from the early Saxon church dedicated to St Pancras. The uncompromising structures of purely functional design failed to complement the city's character. The only artistic aspect of the site is a bronze by the Exeter sculptor Peter Thursby entitled 'Looking Forward'. It was erected on 30 September 1977 to commemorate the Silver Jubilee of Queen Elizabeth II.

A fine Victorian Gothic building was constructed in Waterbeer Street as Exeter's police station and duly opened in 1887. It is seen here in about 1964. Prisoners could be taken straight from the station to the Guildhall opposite for trial. A brick-built structure with a protruding conical tower on the corner of Pancras Lane, this solid building would have made a wonderful focal point for today's shopping centre. The floor of the police station foyer was constructed from a Roman mosaic uncovered and removed from Pancras Lane. The floor was preserved after the demolition of the building, but destroyed when it was wrongly declared a fake.

The site of the old police station is marked by its foundation stone which has been used as a corner stone for a garden.

St Paul's Church and Goldsmith Street, 1949. St Paul's Church situated at the top of Paul Street formed the corner with Goldsmith Street. The church fell into disuse and was removed in 1936. Goldsmith Street was one of the city's most ancient thoroughfares. The rear of the Higher Market is shown with its steps descending into the narrow street. After the removal of the church a restaurant was built on the site; in 1955 it was called Dellers Café.

The site of St Paul's Church, latterly Dellers Café, and Goldsmith Street is now the rear of the Guildhall Shopping Centre in Paul Street. The rebuilding of the shopping centre destroyed any character in the street and made it one of the ugliest in Exeter.

Allhallows' Church, Goldsmith Street, *c*. 1905. The tiny church of Allhallows was one of a number of city parish churches, not to be confused with Allhallows on the Wall. A church existed on the site from the twelfth century. In the early seventeenth century it was enclosed by shops, which were removed in the late nineteenth century. At this point Goldsmith Street was only wide enough to allow a single horse and cart to pass. The church was taken down in 1906 to allow for street widening.

Today there is no trace of the ancient church. A plaque indicating the history of the site does, however, add a little to what is now a rather uninteresting thoroughfare.

The Public Information Bureau, Paul Street, *c.* 1930. The Museum Hotel was removed just after the turn of the century, and the space was later occupied by the Exeter Official Information Bureau. Its role was to inform the public about the city and surrounding areas; it was the forerunner of today's Tourist Information Centre. Information was given free of charge and covered walks, excursions, historical, antiquarian, geological and archaeological interests and everything worth seeing! There was a register where visitors could record suggestions or complaints, and the bureau was also the western district office of the Royal Automobile Club. The building was unlike any other in the city and was an interesting attempt to bring some character to this prominent corner site.

The building of the Harlequin Shopping Centre in the mid-1980s involved rebuilding the corner of Paul Street and Queen Street. The site of the Public Information Bureau is now Chandni Chowk, specialists in foreign clothing, rugs and artefacts.

Paul Street at the junction with Goldsmith Street, *c.* 1960. Before the early 1970s Paul Street still retained a number of old buildings on its south side which gave it scale and character. The building of the Guildhall Shopping Centre in the mid-1970s desecrated the area. The whole south side of Paul Street became a gigantic wall pierced by tunnel-like entrances to loading bays for premises constructed above.

The south side of Paul Street today.

Paul Street and Pancras Lane, 1964. Before the Guildhall Shopping Centre was built, Paul Street contained a number of smaller properties running down its south side. The huge shopping centre decimated the central area between High Street, Paul Street, Queen Street and North Street. The size and inappropriate style of the complex made it an extraordinary development for such a prominent site. The shopping centre virtually removed Goldsmith Street and destroyed Pancras Lane. With vision, earlier buildings could have been retained and incorporated into the new scheme. However, the whole area was to be demolished except for the Higher Market.

Paul Street, where Pancras Lane once entered the street.

5

Magdalen Street, Southernhay & Dix's Field

Southernhay East, with the rebuilt chapel of
Southernhay Congregational church, 2000.

Magdalen Street from the entrance to Southernhay, *c.* 1960. The junction of Magdalen Street, Holloway Street and South Street was almost a village in its own right before its destruction in the late 1970s. There were a number of early properties and buildings of some significance in this area but they did not escape the bulldozer. The postwar creation of Western Way was to give those in power the ideal opportunity to remove many older buildings on the west side of the city. Most of Magdalen Street, the top of Holloway Street and the lower reaches of South Street were swept away. This shows Magdalen Street looking up to the old Eye Infirmary before any changes were made. Now it is totally given over to the motor car. The loss of a group of seventeenth-century houses was tragic.

The Magdalen Street car park today, as seen from the entry to Southernhay. The Eye Infirmary is now empty but there are plans to turn it into a hotel. The conversion of this fine building would appropriately conserve it for the future and retain some character in what is left of lower Magdalen Street.

Magdalen Street looking towards South Street, with original buildings on the north side, *c.* 1960. Joining Southernhay by a gentle curve, the elegant Regency terrace extended to meet a building dating from around 1727 that had been built by one of the city's top surgeons, Dr Dicker. The whole area was obliterated, destroying a charming and historic townscape in 1977.

The site of Dr Dicker's house and the wonderful Regency terrace is today a poorly laid out garden extending up Magdalen Street. The building of a massive hotel has done little for the architectural value of this highly sensitive site.

Magdalen Street at its junction with Holloway Street, showing the north side, *c.* 1960. Magdalen House (Dr Dicker's house) is clearly shown: it is divided in half (note the two colours). Numerous businesses operated in the street. Here, from the left, are Casley the chemist, Castle Dairy, Model Fish Café, A.J. Cox the butcher, a furniture dealer and the City Foot Clinic. The importance of the site prompted later archaeological digs, and new information was gathered on the course of the Civil War in Exeter. Unfortunately the excavations could not take place until the properties were finally removed.

The entrance to Magdalen Street today is a soulless major thoroughfare, with a featureless embankment where fine houses once stood.

The Valiant Soldier Inn, Magdalen Street, 6 April 1959. The junction of South Street, Holloway Street and Magdalen Street comprised a number of historic buildings. Situated on the corner of Holloway Street was this seventeenth-century public house: it was a focal point for the community. Next to the pub was B.R. Warnes, cycle shop, where punctures were quickly mended. In the middle of the street was the railed entrance to underground toilets. Beside it was a granite horse trough with a central pole supported by three dolphins: it was donated to the city by Richard Durant of Sharpham in July 1877. The trough was last seen deposited in a council yard.

It is difficult to relate the site of The Valiant Soldier to the area today. The whole of this part of the city was levelled to create Western Way bypass. An area of great interest and historical note could have added much to Exeter's appeal today. The postwar traffic scheme to the south of the city destroyed an area almost equivalent to that lost in the blitz of May 1942.

Southernhay East, *c.* 1910. This has always been one of the most elegant and desirable areas in Exeter. The photograph shows the Congregational church and part of Southernhay East. The fine Regency terraces have their original railings on the front walls. These railings were removed to aid the Second World War effort. The central property has a canopy extending from the façade over the first-floor balcony. Likewise the balcony on the far right seems to have an additional feature, presumably for keeping off the sun. The church is seen with its original chapel, later to be destroyed in the Exeter blitz of May 1942. Beyond the spire is a balconied Regency building at the entrance to Dix's Field; it was also blitzed.

Southernhay East is shown with the rebuilt chapel of Southernhay Congregational church. Today Southernhay Gardens is open to the public but at one time it was railed off, had entrance gates and was used by residents. These fine Regency terraces are no longer homes but offices, and give businesses one of the most exclusive addresses in the city.

This rare view of Exeter shows Southernhay
Congregational church seen from
Southernhay East in 1906. A fine row of
buildings led from Sidwell Street to
Southernhay without a gap. On the right the
end wall of the Regency terraces that stood at
the top of Southernhay can be seen; they were
lost in the blitz of 1942. The trees denote the
end of the gardens. A fountain once stood in
the gardens opposite the church.

Southernhay Congregational church was
badly damaged in the Second World War
but was then substantially rebuilt. With
the postwar rebuilding of Exeter the elegant
entry into Southernhay East was lost; it is
now a major traffic route.

From the entrance of Dix's Field looking up Southernhay East, *c.* 1930. On the right is the balconied Regency house where the Revd Sabine Baring Gould (author of 'Onward Christian Soldiers') was born. Adjacent to it is the rebuilt Exeter Gaslight & Coke Company. Two fine gas lamps have been placed outside. Southernhay East led directly to High Street.

A new entry created into Southernhay from Paris Street in the postwar period changed the area dramatically. The site of the Exeter Gaslight & Coke Company is now a road junction and car park at the rear of buildings in Paris Street.

Southernhay East, *c.* 1920. During postwar redevelopment the street layout for Paris Street, Sidwell Street and the London Inn Square was altered. The original road leading into Southernhay East was removed. At this time Sidwell Street extended further than it does today, meeting the top of High Street and the London Inn Square. The entry into Southernhay East was from Sidwell Street and it continued to Southernhay Congregational church. It was lined with some interesting buildings. The Regency terraces on the northern side of Southernhay extended past the city wall and can just be seen on the left. The property at the end of the street is in Sidwell Street.

Once an attractive entry into Southernhay East, today the site is partially taken over by car parks for Paris Street businesses.

The entrance to Dix's Field, *c.* 1915. Dix's Field, built in 1805 by Matthew Nosworthy, was one of the most sought after locations in Exeter, formerly for dwellings and latterly for offices. Rows of fine terraces with wrought-iron balconies extended down both sides of a central communal garden. The entrance was embellished with two ironwork lampposts. Buildings in this photograph are occupied by the YWCA. The charity moved to Dix's Field in 1906 setting up an institute home, prayer union branch and bible classes. The hostel housed twenty-one people who paid £1 per week and slept in dormitories of three. The shell of the bombed hostel stood for a considerable period of time before finally being demolished after 1942.

Part of Dix's Field today, in front of the Civic Centre. A considerable section of Dix's Field continued to exist after the bombing in 1942 and the whole complex could easily have been reconstructed. Most remains were demolished and the site left mainly open. The south corner was, however, restored and extended and in latter years incorporated Dix's Field Car Park. The Civic Centre has an unfortunate style of utilitarian architecture that has done nothing to improve the vista of Paris Street.

The birthplace of the Revd Sabine Baring Gould, *c.* 1915. This fine Regency house built in 1809 formed the east side of Dix's Field. Originally a private house, it was later used as a hotel. It was blitzed in 1942.

The east side of Dix's Field entrance today shows the exit into Paris Street, right.

6

Fore Street &
the West Side of Exeter

The Tudor House, 2000.

Fore Street, showing the corner of West Street and the Barton Motor Company, 1932. The clock on the front of the building shows it is 12.17 p.m. To assist customers to see cars a special viewing balcony with decorative railings existed on the corner, with a fine handrail leading down to West Street. The style and grandeur of this building added greatly to the prestige of the street. It was, however, to be demolished and rebuilt, probably not long after this picture was taken. Demolition had started in West Street, where a huge gap had been created.

At the junction of Fore Street and West Street today is a building with far less finesse and a very functional appearance. The site in West Street has been built on and is now a garage.

The top of Fore Street at the junction with St Mary Arches Street, *c.* 1910. Fore Street was much narrower than it is today, buildings were much smaller and there was a great variety of architecture created over a long period of time. On the left the original narrow entrance to St Mary Arches Street can be seen, and opposite the frontage of the Lower Market can just be made out. At this time there were no electric trams and all traffic was horse drawn.

The top of Fore Street was subject to extensive war damage and the Lower Market was gutted. The shell of the market building remained for a long time after the war and its style was unique in the city. It was replaced by St George's Hall. The top of Fore Street was opened up and the street greatly widened. Like upper High Street its intimate character was lost. St Mary Arches Street today is a major through route and what was an intriguing old street now has little to commend it.

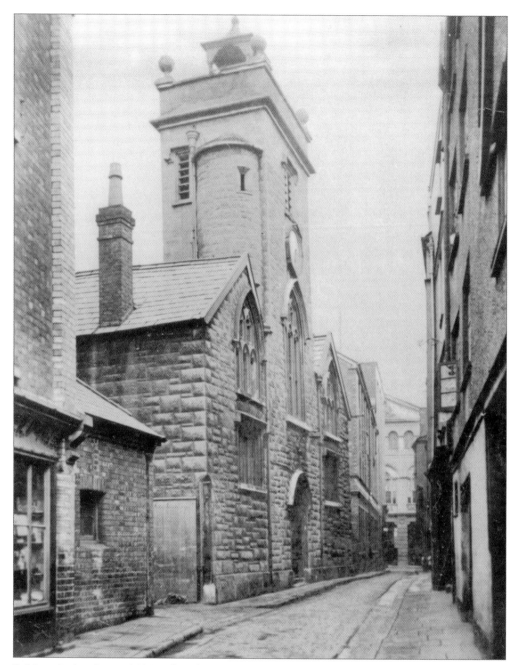

St Mary Arches Street, 1930s. This photograph shows the narrowness of one of Exeter's older back streets. The focal point of the street, St Mary Arches Church, was the civic church for Exeter. The plain exterior gives no indication that the building contains a fine Norman arched interior with numerous wall memorials, inscriptions and tablets dedicated to past mayors and dignitaries. Entry on the south side was through a simple iron gate and there were tombstones on the outside of the church. All have disappeared. The building was rendered with plaster at the turn of the century. The tower supports four balls taken from the water conduit in South Street after it was demolished in 1834. A bell turret also existed at this time. At the end of the street can be seen the façade of the Lower Market, built in 1834, in Fore Street.

Today St Mary Arches Street is approximately three times wider than it was before the Second World War and its character has been mostly destroyed. The street was subject to war damage and then demolition. The church and a few buildings at the north end are all that remains of the original street. Facing the street is St George's Hall, the replacement for the Civic Hall in Queen Street, which was removed in the building of the Guildhall Shopping Centre in the 1970s. St George's Hall was constructed on the site of the Lower Market, whose blitzed ruins were demolished. St Mary Arches Street is now dominated by a car park, pubs and nightclubs and is a major traffic thoroughfare.

A lady enjoys a stroll up Quay Lane in the 1930s. Note the open gutter running down the hill.

Walking in the steps of the past, a gentleman comes up from the Quay. There are fine views over the surrounding countryside. The wisdom of destroying all the old buildings on Quay Lane must be questioned as nothing of significance now occupies this barren site. Their reconstruction could recreate a fascinating route to the Quay.

In 1927 an extraordinary incident occurred when a section of the city wall fell on the Custom House Inn, which stood at the bottom of Quay Hill. The building was so damaged that it had to be demolished. To prevent a repetition of the accident, building was not allowed within a fixed distance of the wall. In the last fifteen years far more attention has been paid to the city's ancient wall and it is now more accessible to the public than ever before.

Quay Lane was for many Exeter people a quaint shortcut to the Quay from the top of Holloway Street. Its top entrance was a narrow alley and could be easily missed. The delightful hill had a number of small cottages running its whole length and gardens ending at the city wall. It was said that one could pass from one cottage to the other without coming out of any building!

Coombe Street from Quay Hill, *c.* 1910. Before the Second World War Coombe Street was a small but busy access route leading directly to the Quay from South Street. It was lined with buildings on both sides and was a focal point for the community because an entrance to Central School ran off it. Coombe Street was also connected to James Street. A number of businesses operated in this street, including in the 1950s Moreland's Match Manufacturers, Chudley Stationery, St Thomas Rural Meat Co., and the Motor Cycle Exchange. The White Hart Hotel yard and stables were also a feature of the street. The south tower of the cathedral is visible and West Street starts on the left at the bottom of the photograph.

The creation of Western Way inner bypass in 1969 was carried out at the expense of Coombe Street, dividing it in half. Lower Coombe Street (as it is now called) leads to the entrance of the new Cathedral and Quay Car Park, opened in 1993. In this picture the entrance is hidden by trees. The road construction involved the demolition of numerous buildings and the infilling of central Coombe Street to a depth of approximately 10ft. A pedestrian subway now links the two parts of the street. Today the lower part of the street is unrecognisable from the earlier photograph.

In 1970 five cottages still overlooked the Higher Leat at Cricklepit Mill. Known as Leat Terrace, they were a charming example of early nineteenth-century cottages for workers who would have earned their living in the adjacent area of Shilhay. It was the main industrial area in the city and residents could have been employed at the mill next door, the foundries, tanneries or candle factory. Nearby was Tremlett's Tannery, the biggest business of its type in the city, opposite St Edmund's church. The remains of Exeter's medieval bridge formed Edmund Street and St Edmund's church still stood at this date.

The site of Leat Terrace is now the outside drinking area for The Bishop Blaize pub and the area beyond is given over to a car park behind Exe Bridge House. The building was constructed for British Telecommunications, which still operates there today.

Historically the area known as the West Quarter was centred around West Street and included a number of older back streets. It was in this area that many of the city's workers lived. Conditions were often poor but the community spirit good. This photograph dates from around 1910 and shows the bottom of Stepcote Hill and its adjoining buildings. A horse and cart stands outside E. Pearse & Co., rag and bone merchants.

The area of West Street and Stepcote Hill forms one of Exeter's historical and architectural gems and yet the city fails to promote the area. This group of buildings, including St Mary Steps Church, 'The House That Moved' and the timber-framed properties at the bottom of Stepcote Hill, form one of the most charming scenes in the city yet visitors only come across them by accident. A scheme proposed by the Exeter Civic Society in 1980 suggested landscaping the area and creating an historical focal point. It would have meant banning car parking but this was thought to be unacceptable. So we have to contend with cars blocking the view of some of Exeter's most famous buildings. Tourist potential is being lost.

St Mary Steps Church and old houses in West Street, *c.* 1920. Here, in one of Exeter's most famous areas, artists came to capture the charm of the ancient buildings, church and Stepcote Hill. On the left is a property demolished in the early 1940s. It was to become the site for 'The House that Moved' in 1961. Ironically, the demolished building was of the same period as its replacement! The buildings on the right were in poor condition at the time this photograph was taken, but the two medieval properties were to be restored in the 1930s and luckily escaped demolition.

One of Exeter's most important historic areas is today given over to the car. In 1961 the empty site at West Gate was filled by a building that originally stood on the corner of Edmund Street and Frog Street. The operation to move it attracted worldwide publicity and it was to become a famous attraction. There is nothing to relate this extraordinary story to the many visitors who stray this way today. The combination of timber-framed buildings, a medieval cobbled hill, the site of one of the city's gates and a house that was picked up and moved have all the elements required to promote Exeter's historic past, but a golden opportunity is being missed.

The corner of West Gate, *c.* 1930, showing the original property that stood on the site. It probably dated from the fifteenth or sixteenth century. The rendered timber-framed structure oversailed the street, a typical feature of these early buildings. At the rear of the building are the remains of the City Wall and West Gate. Additions were made to the property with galvanised iron extensions to the rear. Another interesting period building next door completes the historic corner site. The restoration of these properties would have added greatly to this famous local area.

In 1961 no. 16 Edmund Street was lifted from its site after being encased in a wooden structure and winched on rails to West Street. Its new site was that of the building shown above. The previous structure was razed to the ground in the early 1940s. Fully restored, 'The House that Moved' has had a number of owners and is currently a wedding dress shop.

West Street and its old houses were recognised as an attraction at the turn of the century as this postcard, dated 1909, shows. The group of buildings created an attractive frontage to the entrance to the city via Stepcote Hill. The area of the West Quarter was occupied by working people but in earlier times had been the home of wealthy merchants who traded from the Quay and adjacent areas. Exeter was to retain some merchant's buildings until very early in the twentieth century. The three buildings shown to the right have been removed but the properties to the left were restored in the 1930s. A number of residents and children are shown in the street and a lady in a long skirt and with black hat is removing large wicker baskets from a four-wheel horse-drawn cart.

West Street, with the two restored buildings and a lamppost now standing at the bottom of Stepcote Hill. It is suggested that this gas light fitting is just a decorative feature and not in a style reminiscent of the early Exeter lampposts found in this quarter. The character of the street is marred by inappropriate shopfronts to the right of the picture.

This view taken in about 1915 from the middle of Stepcote Hill shows buildings in need of restoration. The buildings on the left were restored in the 1930s but the two premises on the right were removed, spoiling the continuity of the street.

Stepcote Hill, March 2000.

Stepcote Hill from the Sunday School, *c.* 1915. The buildings on the right were to be restored but buildings at the top of the hill were demolished.

While Stepcote Hill has been substantially altered in its upper section the street is still a remarkable survivor. With appropriate promotion and interpretation far more could be done to bring this unique street to the public's attention.

Medieval Stepcote Hill was originally designed to accommodate packhorses and pedestrians. The open gutter led up to Smythen Street, at one time the street of the butchers (Butchers Row). The slaughtering of animals and gutting required the street to be cleaned: blood and organs could flow down over Stepcote Hill. Here we see a large group of children using the hill as their playground overseen by two ladies. Child mortality was high. Interestingly there are six buckets standing on the hill. A number of the properties possibly did not have sufficient sanitary facilities and there are stories of police officers having 'chamber pots' emptied over them while they carried out their duties.

A slum clearance scheme in the 1930s removed many of the West Quarter's residents and Stepcote Hill was substantially demolished. While living standards were improved by new housing, the hill was radically altered and much of its earlier character has been lost.

Left: No. 16 Edmund Street, an early fifteenth-century house, occupied a prominent site on the junction with Frog Street. The street is recognised from the earliest times and the house, on its corner site, was known to many people in Exeter. It is shown before attempts at restoration in the 1930s. The timber-framed property oversailed the street. Two children are playing outside, while a pram is parked outside the front door and some underwear is attached the boarded up front. A shop once existed on the ground floor. A further storey had been added to the building at some point and is seen above the main gable. In the 1950s the property was threatened with demolition but a preservation order saved it. In 1961 the building was removed from its original site, on rails, to a new site on the corner of West Street. Today it is known as 'The House that Moved'. *Above*: The site of 16 Edmund Street is today in the middle of a traffic island, and the whole of Frog Street and its adjacent areas have been radically altered.

Frog Street, *c.* 1960. Frog Street, a narrow and ancient thoroughfare, led from Edmund Street to the entrance of Exe Island and New Bridge Street. This view looks up to New Bridge Street, which is the elevated road in the centre of the picture. The heavily buttressed walls supporting New Bridge Street were constructed in 1770s and to the right of the wall is part of the arch which was the entrance to Exe Island. On the right stands a simple timber-framed building dating from the sixteenth century. It was demolished together with the rest of the street in 1961.

Frog Street no longer exists. The concrete replacement for the Exe Island entrance has destroyed what was a fascinating aspect of New Bridge Street. The ancient area of Exe Island has also undergone dramatic changes – most of its buildings have been removed.

A rare etching by the gifted artist the late Miss Hayman shows the end of Tudor Street as it turns to enter Bonhay Road, *c.* 1930. Scenes like this existed in many parts of the city pre-war. Small groups of cottages such as these would today be regarded as an important part of the city's heritage. Sadly, however, they were demolished. The church tower shown is that of Allhallows' Church in Bartholomew Yard, removed in 1950.

Tudor Street today has mostly lost its significance except for the Tudor House and some adjacent properties. The area has been transformed by the construction of large storage buildings.

A shepherd driving sheep to market along Bonhay Road, *c.* 1915. The street led to the city's livestock market and this photograph shows a shepherd driving his flock to the market entrance. On the left are the evergreen oaks flanking the market. Dominating the end of the road on the right is the four-storeyed ice factory. It was destroyed by fire early in the twentieth century. The factory supplied many businesses across the city, including pubs, restaurants and the meat trade, with ice blocks. This is probably the only surviving photograph of the building. The Exeter company of F. Parkin & Sons is advertised on the roadside premises. Parkin's Foundry was a long-established firm on Exe Island.

Bonhay Road still retains the evergreen oaks that were part of the old livestock market site. The Lower Leat running from the mill on the Exe is now culverted and the area still retains industrial units, now for storage.

Until the 1960s the route into Exeter from the west was completely different from today. Crossing the single-arch steel Exe bridge, travellers turned right to West Street, leading to Coombe Street and South Street. This view shows the start of West Street from the end of Edmund Street. The railings, right, indicate a significant drop. The two timber-framed black-and-white buildings are at the bottom of West Street and the foot of Stepcote Hill.

Edmund Street and its adjacent area no longer exist. The whole site was bulldozed to make way for Western Way inner bypass and the construction of two new Exe bridges. The historical significance of the approach into Exeter from the west might have provided a great opportunity to create a fascinating new entrance to the city. The actual development created a landscape where no historic structure was left standing except the tower of St Edmund's Church and the remains of Exeter's medieval bridge, which, unfortunately, is well below the raised level of the surrounding area.

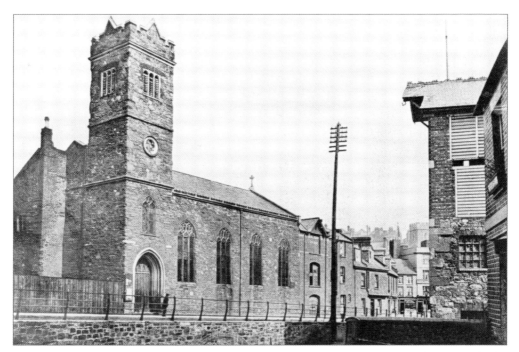

St Edmund's Church, *c.* 1910. Rebuilt in the fifteenth and nineteenth centuries, the church had a prominent position on Exeter's medieval stone bridge. When a new bridge was built on a different line in the eighteenth century, the partially demolished medieval bridge was retained as a road and took its name from the church of St Edmund. The road was a fascinating route into the city. Opposite the church is Tremlett's Tannery. All these buildings were demolished with the construction of Western Way in the 1960s and the church mostly removed, with the exception of part of the tower.

The remains of the city's medieval bridge were uncovered and retained but the church of St Edmund was mostly demolished, leaving only the tower to indicate its former presence. The site was supposed to create an attractive ruin but its southern side is so highly banked it cannot be seen from the road. It is today a forgotten and unexplained site and is worthy of far more attention by the city. The route into Exeter from the west across this national monument is a prominent aspect of Exeter's history and yet visitors and residents have little to inform them of the importance of the site.

Edmund Street before its destruction in the 1960s. All buildings were demolished and most of the church was pulled down: its ancient foundations were left open to view. The road surface was dug up to expose the substantial remains of the multi-arched medieval bridge. Exeter's twelfth-century stone bridge is a national monument now, on view in landscaped surroundings.

The ancient Edmund Street no longer exists but the remains of the early stone bridge are retained within a landscaped area surrounded by busy traffic routes.

In 1979 the fourteenth-century The Bishop Blaize pub became known as Nosey Parkers. The name provoked criticism as this was the oldest public house outside the city wall and had firm connections with the woollen cloth trade. Eventually its original name was restored. Cricklepit Mill is shown in its original state in this 1987 photograph. It was the last surviving working mill in Exeter. Adjacent to it is the 90-ft long cloth drying shed. The mill was powered by water from the Higher Leat which flowed through the middle of the building and drove its huge wooden water wheels. The property was sold by its owners W.G. Shears.

The historic site, which should have been purchased by the local authority, was left to fall into disrepair. An opportunity to retain the city's heritage was lost when Cricklepit Mill was destroyed by fire in 1999. Ironically, within a matter of days the destroyed mill was covered with plastic and scaffold poles to preserve the gutted ruins. The destruction of Cricklepit Mill is a familiar story, showing an attitude of complacency and lack of interest in Exeter's heritage. This site is now being developed as a centre for young homeless people.

The burnt-out ruin of Cricklepit Mill, March 2000.

Exe Island Lodging House, 1963. The area of Exe Island was dominated by this large Heavitree stone building, clearly seen from New Bridge Street. It was almost opposite the Tudor House. Known as the Exe Island Lodging House or Reception Centre, it was managed by Exeter City Council. The substantial nature of the building suggests that it was formerly built for a more significant purpose, probably a warehouse as this area was one of the city's commercial centres. In the past gasworks, abattoir and market all existed in the vicinity.

In 1948 the City Council took over the running of the Exe Island Reception Centre and operated it on behalf of the National Assistance Board. In 1957 the centre ran into problems when a huge influx of homeless and destitute men began to use the facilities. It is recorded that 2,671 admissions took place in three months. After 1969 the building was demolished.

No. 11 West Street (built *c*. 1500) occupied by S. Gridland, *c*. 1910. The wooden framework of the original structure can be clearly seen and on its north side is a large notice board facing Stepcote Hill. At the bottom of the hill is what appears to be a water hydrant with a drinking bowl. A notice in the window advertises beds. About thirty years later these buildings were well restored.

Threatened with demolition in the 1930s, 11 and 12 West Street were retained and restored. Today these two properties continue to add to the ambience of this historic corner of Exeter. The buildings have been renumbered.

In 1960 the curious visitor to Exe Island and Tudor Street would have come across a derelict building which had obvious historic merit. The building occupied by the Tudor Electrical Company is in poor condition but still has its first-floor slate hangings bearing coats of arms. It is said that these date from the 1820s. The property was built in the early seventeenth century for a maltster; it has survived thanks to the tenacity of a single individual, Bill Lovell.

The Tudor House, as it is now called, was purchased by restorer Bill Lovell in 1963, and with great dedication he spent twelve years restoring it. Wherever possible, original methods of construction were adhered to with the result that the property was completely resurrected. It was offered to Exeter City Council for £45,000, to be retained as part of the city's heritage, but was refused. It gives a wonderful idea of the buildings of Exeter's past but today is largely forgotten. As this book went to print, it was for sale for £350,000.

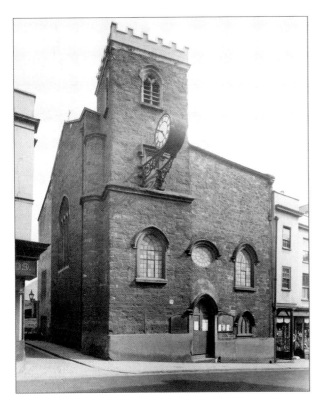

St John's Church, Fore Street, *c.* 1920. St John's Church was a prominent feature in Fore Street and the side of the church formed part of John Street. The Heavitree stone-built church had been subject to numerous alterations during its lifetime, including the removal of its arch and chancel in 1864. Its fine clock was illuminated at night: the locals called it the 'moon of Fore Street'. The church was removed partially in 1864; demolition work continued until 1957 when the tower was removed.

The rebuilt site of St John's Church, March 2000, now operating as Taunton Leisure outdoor clothing specialists.

Property in Mint Lane, 1938. Leaving Fore Street and entering Mint Lane, at the rear of the Mint Tavern there is a structure which is both interesting and surprising, for within its small walled garden is a well. Water sources incorporated in dwellings are found elsewhere in the city and some of the wells are very ancient. The building, probably seventeenth-century, has been sensitively restored and adds to the charm of this small back street. The oriel windows are supported by three carved brackets. The city had numerous timber-framed properties, with courtyards and alleyway, but many of these were to be removed in the postwar period.

The retention of older buildings adds to the character of this back lane.

The Old Chevalier Inn, Fore Street, 1940. A fine pair of seventeenth-century houses of outstanding historical merit stood at the top of Fore Street. Latterly known as the Old Chevalier Inn, the building took its name from an equestrian statue that stood on one of the gables. In the earlier part of the twentieth century the properties were threatened with demolition but were saved by the city. The architect James Crocker commended these buildings in his book *Old Exeter* published in the 1880s, stating they were some of the finest examples in the city. Latterly wine and spirit merchants operated from 78 and 79 Fore Street, as well as a bookshop. In 1940 the two buildings were integrated and became the Old Chevalier Inn. The life of the public house was short as it was destroyed during the blitz of May 1942.

The site of the Chevalier Inn is still a venue for entertainment, but its style and ambience have changed beyond recognition.

The Mint Chapel, Fore Street, *c.* 1920. Before the 1960s the handsome Mint Chapel could be seen at the top of Fore Street. Built in 1813, it replaced a former chapel. The new building was constructed, at considerable cost, by the Wesleyan Methodists. The balconied interior with box pews and a central pulpit entered by a fine wrought-iron staircase added to the quality of the building.

The modern Mint Methodist church, opened in 1970. The old burial ground that surrounded the old chapel was closed in 1867, but tombstones can still be seen propped up against the boundary wall.

The demolition of Follett's Building and Mermaid Yard, 1979. Mermaid Yard on the south side of the old West Quarter was once the site of the Mermaid Inn. The large public house overlooked the river and is recorded as being in existence in 1632. The prime site was, however, to be built on and in 1874 the Improved Industrial Dwellings Company of Exeter opened a tenement block and named it after the Chief Magistrate, Follett's Buildings. A further development of cottages on three sides formed a square. Follett's Buildings had excellent views over the River Exe. Housing a number of local families, it had a character all its own. The substantial brick buildings were demolished in the 1970s, and this photograph shows the work nearly complete in 1979.

Follett's Buildings and Cotton's Buildings could have been adapted for the modern age to retain the area's character. The new buildings on the site, while providing good accommodation, have little architectural merit.

7

The Cathedral Close,
South Street,
Kalendarhay &
Catherine Street

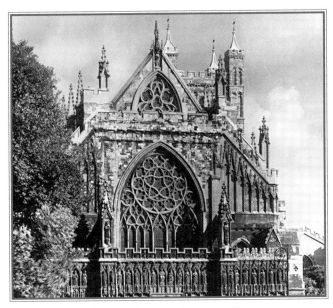

The Cathedral west front, *c.* 1920.

South Street entrance to the Vicars Choral Hall,
c. 1920. Before the Second World War a fine hall
existed halfway down South Street on the east side.
Dating from the fourteenth century, it had a
splendid panelled sixteenth-century interior. The
hall was part of an extensive complex known as the
Vicars Choral. Two rows of cottages with a fine
cathedral yard entrance had been created in the
fourteenth century to house priests. The college
ended at South Street with the communal hall in
this photograph. Latterly there was an entrance on
South Street. The College of the Vicars Choral was
one of the city's important architectural gems. The
hall was in use right up until the Second World War.

The ruin of the Vicars Choral Hall is
today retained as a memorial to those
who died in the Exeter blitz in May 1942.
The building destroyed in the war should
have an interpretation panel to explain
its history to the public. In 1999 the
Dean and Chapter railed its exterior to
protect it from vandalism.

The rear entrance of the Vicars Choral Hall from Kalendarhay, 1930s.

The site of the Vicars Choral Hall rear entrance, also showing rebuilt postwar buildings in South Street.

The interior of Vicars Choral Hall, c. 1930.

A view of the College of the Vicars Choral looking east shows the entrance gate with the gable of the west front of Exeter Cathedral behind, *c.* 1830. The gatehouse was to be demolished in 1872 and all the existing buildings, with the exception of the hall, were removed by 1900.

The view from Kalendarhay today gives no indication that a remarkable complex once existed on the site.

The Globe Hotel, Cathedral Yard, *c.* 1930. One of Exeter's most prestigious pre-war hotels stood in the corner of the Cathedral Yard adjacent to St Petrock's Church. The seventeenth-century building was a charming aspect of Cathedral Yard and access to South Street was possible by passing through its main entrance. The curving building led directly to Little Stile, one of the ancient gates to the Yard, which is just visible far left. The front entrance with its simple porch was Georgian, and in the 1930s the hotel's interior still reflected the time when it was one of the primary coaching inns in the city.

In May 1942 the Globe Hotel was totally gutted in the Exeter blitz and the remains of the hotel and adjacent buildings up to High Street had to be removed. The postwar rebuilding of the top of South Street took little account of the neighbouring historic buildings, and today this important access to Exeter's prime tourist area is lacking in elegance and style.

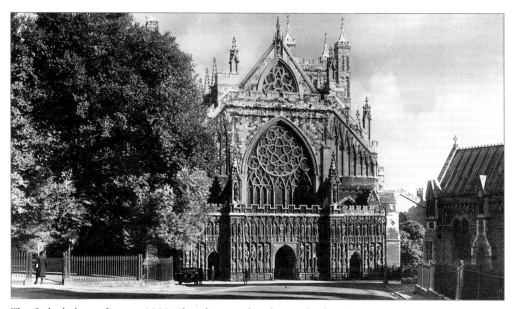

The Cathedral west front, *c.* 1920. This photograph indicates the discolouring that had taken place over the centuries. The deterioration of the stone has been attributed to pollution from coal fires, traditional bonfires, and latterly the Second World War. Restoration has been a constant problem for the Dean and Chapter. The side of St Mary Major's Church is shown on the right.

Over the last thirty years an enormous programme of restoration has been undertaken at Exeter Cathedral and has included the cleaning of the whole of the west front. The operation facilitated further historical investigations into the famous screen. Today it has plain stone images, but the medieval screen and its figures were originally painted with vibrant colours. Conservators painstakingly gathered minute samples of paint found on the screen and its images and brilliantly recreated the screen as it would have been seen in medieval times. It was a remarkable piece of work and gave a completely new insight into the famous building. St Mary Major's Church was demolished in 1971. The removal of the railings around the Close for the war effort proved unnecessary as the metal was substandard and could not be used. Today the reintroduction of some railings is being considered to combat vandalism.

The Cathedral Yard, from where the Globe Hotel (blitzed 1942) stood, *c.* 1910. On the left is the façade of the City Bank, completed in 1877. A fine coat of arms above the impressive doorway bears the date and words 'City Bank est. 1786'. The building was constructed in two parts and was extended on to the frontage of High Street in 1905.

The old City Bank building is today occupied by the Halifax Building Society and railings no longer surround the Cathedral Yard and Close. Parking is strictly limited here and the road that once led to the west front of the Cathedral is now a pedestrian processional way. In recent times new trees have been planted to take the place of the lost Dutch elms. The corner site, 2 Broad Gate, is still called Tinleys after the restaurant and tea rooms that operated here from 1932 to 1992.

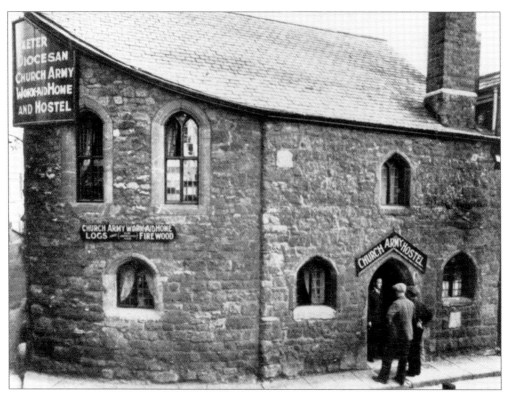

This delightful picture from the 1930s shows the Church Army Hostel in Catherine Street which occupied the medieval St Catherine's almshouses. The Church Army functioned continuously here from 1894. Between January and 31 December 1895 sixty-one men passed through the hostel. During 1931–2 204 men were admitted. No man was refused shelter and the home operated a work aid method. Food and shelter were supplied and if the recipient did one hour's work he obtained breakfast. If he was mentally and physically fit he could remain, room permitting, for not more than four months, and all help would be given to place him in a regular job. Prayers were said in the tiny chapel. Work entailed the collection of wood and sawing logs for sale, as advertised on the front of the building. The hostel operated up to the Second World War. (*Church Army*)

Blitzed in 1942, the ruin of the fifteenth-century St Catherine's almshouses were landscaped and retained as a memorial. However, the history of the site is not strongly apparent to those viewing it today. Although a scheme of interpretation panels was instigated by the City Council, they have failed to stand up to persistent vandalism.

South Street at the junction with Bear Street, *c.* 1960. The Exeter blitz uncovered some of Exeter's lost heritage and at this junction stood a large stone tower that was completely exposed by the destruction of surrounding buildings. The actual origins of the tower were obscure but it was obviously an important structure, perhaps linked to the old Bear Gate leading to the Cathedral Yard. Constructed from Heavitree stone, Bear Tower was thought to have dated from the fifteenth century because it was typical of many other buildings of that period in the city. Latterly the tower had been integrated into a shop. After being exposed it was left standing for twenty-four years.

Bear Tower, although a ruin, was a feature of ancient Bear Street but, in 1965 the City Council received permission to remove it. A plaque was inserted into the pavement to recall its presence and the site was used for parking. What could have been an interesting corner was lost.

The butcher's at South Street, *c.* 1910. One of Exeter's early timber-framed buildings was portrayed in a lantern slide, which clearly shows that the premises in South Street next to the White Hart Hotel was a butcher's shop on the ground floor. It remained so for much of the twentieth century and will be recalled by Exonians from the area as Reynolds the butchers. It is shown here as an open-fronted property with carcasses hanging up on rails. The fronts were boarded at night. Next door is Palmer & Co., the bakers. Many owners lived above their shops, which maintained the social life of the city.

No. 67 South Street is today a well-maintained historic building. While the first and second floors are in keeping with the period, the current occupiers have chosen an unfortunate colour scheme of dark blue for the shopfront which is totally alien to the character of the building. The large functional lettering used for the company name also clashes with the period building. The local authority produces guidelines for such situations and it would be appropriate to offer further assistance to ensure the building's qualities are maintained.

8
Quay & Canal

Exeter Quay, *c.* 1900.

Exeter Quay from Haven Banks, *c.* 1910. At this time two vessels were moored in front of the warehouses. On the left (Shilhay), timber storage yards are shown with large piles of wood seasoning. On Haven Banks (right) timber is ready to be removed and a horse is waiting, patiently attached to a wagon. The riverside site of Haven Banks was a favourite venue for the city's fairs.

Exeter's riverside and Quay underwent dramatic change from the 1960s onwards. The essential flood prevention scheme effectively harnessed the river, preventing drastic inundation. The scheme concreted extensive areas of the river's edge, creating a channel but losing the feel of a rural waterway. The Quay and adjoining areas have been subject to restoration and changes of use for leisure and housing, but lack any major attraction.

The area opposite the old Electricity Generating Station is shown here in 1987 before a large development of apartments and some retail outlets. Haven Banks has been almost totally given over to housing. An area that could have been a real focal point for major tourism attractions and cultural activities has been virtually lost. There has been much criticism relating to the development of the riverside area and in particular the loss of the Maritime Museum, Exeter's only real large-scale attraction.

The new Haven Banks development.

King's Arms Sluice, *c.* 1910. The Exeter Ship Canal is the oldest pound-lock canal in England and the view above looks from King's Arms Sluice towards the city. The lock-keeper's cottage is on the right: it was removed in 1969. The creation of the canal brought a great deal of wealth to Exeter and gave seagoing ships direct access to the city. It has been the responsibility of the local authority for over 400 years.

Recognised as one of the largest stretches of fresh water in the South-West, the Exeter Ship Canal and its adjacent habitats are one of the most important conservation areas in the south-west. The 5¼-mile canal with its towpath is a walker's delight. Today the canal is hardly used and not sufficiently promoted as one of Exeter's leisure assets. Most visitors coming to the city are not aware that such a facility exists, and in these days of eco-tourism opportunities are being lost.

Exeter Quay with the hand-operated ferry making its way across the River Exe, *c*. 1900. In front of the fine early nineteenth-century warehouses are four horse-drawn wagons taking on board stone which had been deposited on the quay. Stone and bricks were often used as ballast in ships. The port declined and over the next eighty years became derelict but still retained much of its character.

From the mid-1980s the Quay was viewed as a potential tourist mecca for Exeter and it was thought that the area would put the city on the map. Despite the restoration and refurbishment of the area, this has not transpired. The main tourist attraction, the Maritime Museum created in the 1960s, has been lost and to date no other major attraction has taken its place.

The creation of the Basin at the head of the Exeter Ship Canal, opened in 1830, provided better facilities for vessels bringing goods into the city. A special train siding allowed wagons to be placed beside vessels, as seen here. Special turntables were constructed at each corner at the head of the Basin to allow the wagons to pass down the side. The turntable bases are still visible today. Part of the warehouses was the business premises of Mitchell & Son, building material merchants, seen here in about 1910. Products were removed by horse-drawn wagons and a pulley is being used to drop goods straight into the wagon below. The corrugated-iron structure, an extension to the original building, allowed entry for wagons at the rear of the building.

In the latter part of the twentieth century the old warehouses on the Basin housed part of the Exeter Maritime Museum. The departure of the museum in 1997 has been one of the most controversial issues in the city in recent years and the City Council is now struggling to find an answer to the redevelopment of the Basin.

Exeter Quay, seen here in about 1905, was built beside red sandstone cliffs and provided an excellent facility for shipping goods to the city. The view was taken from opposite Colleton Hill looking upstream. Below Colleton Crescent on its cliff top site can be seen a row of warehouses. Deposited on the Quay are large quantities of scrap iron and even a small steam traction engine. The material was taken from this site as ballast in ships and sold on the continent. The Quay at this time still had the feeling of a working port.

Exeter Quay today is totally geared towards leisure and housing with some retail outlets. The cliff face has been mostly cleared of vegetation. Just below the top wall a small path which was once used by a nightwatchman still exists. He looked after shipping moored at the Quay. The old warehouses at the end of the Quay have been removed and replaced by housing, decorative lamps and bollards.

The Basin at its entrance to King's Arms Sluice with a group of children carrying wicker baskets, *c.* 1910. The area was very much the territory of working vessels: two ships are moored on the east side. A simple hand-cranked crane is standing on the edge of the Basin to help with the loading of timber in piles beside it. On the far right is a haystack for feeding the horses that towed vessels up the canal.

The Basin today is not a commercial working area for shipping but there are still individuals who repair their vessels here. It is now being viewed for redevelopment with possible further building around the perimeter of the Basin. The last remnants of Exeter's maritime past will probably disappear.

ACKNOWLEDGEMENTS

I would like to thank the staff of the Devon and Exeter Institution for their help and assistance. I am indebted also to the staff of the West Country Studies Library for their diligence, knowledge and support. I acknowledge the *Express and Echo* for their long-term policy of publishing local history articles.

To Mr R. Dunsford of Leare, Brown and Dunsford of Exeter I am most grateful for the use of photographs and also Messrs Bruford & Son for use of company records. I express my sincere thanks to David Milton for his help and interest. I am also most grateful to the Church Army and their officer for help and material supplied. To Eric Cleave for your support. For allowing a vantage point in the city, my thanks to Boots the Chemist and its manager Alan Mutton. For continued support, help, guidance and checking I thank my friend Lorna.

Lastly, I should like to thank my publishers, Sutton Publishing, for their support and continuing enthusiasm for producing works on Exeter.